# Key Facts™ on Venezuela

*~Essential Information on Venezuela~*

By Patrick W. Nee

The Internationalist®
www.internationalist.com

**The Internationalist®**

*International Business, Investment, and Travel*

**Published by:**

The Internationalist Publishing Company

96 Walter Street/ Suite 200

Boston, MA 02131, USA

Tel: 617-354-7722

www.internationalist.com

PN@internationalist.com

Copyright © 2013 by PWN

The Internationalist is a Registered Trademark. "Key Facts" and "The Internationalist Business Guides" are Trademarks of The Internationalist Publishing Company.

All Rights are reserved under International, Pan-American, and Pan-Asian Conventions. No part of this book may be reproduced in any form without the written permission of the publisher. All rights vigorously enforced

# *Table Of Contents*

Chapter 1: Background

Chapter 2: Geography

Chapter 3: People and Society

Chapter 4: Government and Key Leaders

Chapter 5: Economy

Chapter 6: Energy

Chapter 7: Communications

Chapter 8: Transportation

Chapter 9: Military

Chapter 10: Transnational Issues

Map of Venezuela

# Chapter 1: Background

Venezuela was one of three countries that emerged from the collapse of Gran Colombia in 1830 (the others being Ecuador and New Granada, which became Colombia). For most of the first half of the 20th century, Venezuela was ruled by generally benevolent military strongmen, who promoted the oil industry and allowed for some social reforms. Democratically elected governments have held sway since 1959. Hugo CHAVEZ, president from 1999 to 2013, sought to implement his "21st Century Socialism," which purported to alleviate social ills while at the same time attacking capitalist globalization and existing democratic institutions. Current concerns include: a weakening of democratic institutions, political polarization, a politicized military, rampant violent crime, overdependence on the petroleum industry with its price fluctuations, and irresponsible mining operations that are endangering the rain forest and indigenous peoples.

## Chapter 2: Geography

**Location:**
>Northern South America, bordering the Caribbean Sea and the North Atlantic Ocean, between Colombia and Guyana

**Geographic coordinates:**
>8 00 N, 66 00 W

**Map references:**
>South America

**Area:**
>total: 912,050 sq km
>
>country comparison to the world: 33
>
>land: 882,050 sq km
>
>water: 30,000 sq km

**Area - comparative:**
>slightly more than twice the size of California

**Land boundaries:**
>total: 4,993 km
>
>border countries: Brazil 2,200 km, Colombia 2,050 km, Guyana 743 km

**Coastline:**
>2,800 km

**Maritime claims:**

territorial sea: 12 nm

contiguous zone: 15 nm

exclusive economic zone: 200 nm

continental shelf: 200 m depth or to the depth of exploitation

**Climate:**

tropical; hot, humid; more moderate in highlands

**Terrain:**

Andes Mountains and Maracaibo Lowlands in northwest; central plains (llanos); Guiana Highlands in southeast

**Elevation extremes:**

lowest point: Caribbean Sea 0 m

highest point: Pico Bolivar 5,007 m

**Natural resources:**

petroleum, natural gas, iron ore, gold, bauxite, other minerals, hydropower, diamonds

**Land use:**

arable land: 2.85%

permanent crops: 0.71%

other: 96.44% (2011)

**Irrigated land:**

10,550 sq km (2008)

**Total renewable water resources:**

1,233 cu km (2011)

**Freshwater withdrawal (domestic/industrial/agricultural):**

 total: 9.06 cu km/yr (23%/4%/74%)

 per capita: 358.6 cu m/yr (2008)

**Natural hazards:**

 subject to floods, rockslides, mudslides; periodic droughts

**Environment - current issues:**

 sewage pollution of Lago de Valencia; oil and urban pollution of Lago de Maracaibo; deforestation; soil degradation; urban and industrial pollution, especially along the Caribbean coast; threat to the rainforest ecosystem from irresponsible mining operations

**Environment - international agreements:**

 party to: Antarctic Treaty, Biodiversity, Climate Change, Climate Change-Kyoto Protocol, Desertification, Endangered Species, Hazardous Wastes, Marine Life Conservation, Ozone Layer Protection, Ship Pollution, Tropical Timber 83, Tropical Timber 94, Wetlands

 signed but not ratified:: none of the selected agreements

**Geography - note:**

on major sea and air routes linking North and South America; Angel Falls in the Guiana Highlands is the world's highest waterfall

# Chapter 3: People and Society

**Nationality:**

noun: Venezuelan(s)

adjective: Venezuelan

**Ethnic groups:**

Spanish, Italian, Portuguese, Arab, German, African, indigenous people

**Languages:**

Spanish (official), numerous indigenous dialects

**Religions:**

nominally Roman Catholic 96%, Protestant 2%, other 2%

**Demographic profile:**

Although poverty in Venezuela has declined during the CHAVEZ administration, dropping from nearly 50% in 1999 to about 27% in 2011, it remains high and some experts question how much of a role social expenditures have played in this poverty reduction. Progress in lowering poverty, income inequality, and unemployment may in fact be more closely linked to the rise and fall of prices for oil, Venezuela's dominant export. In the long-run, education and healthcare spending may increase economic growth and reduce income inequality, but rising costs and the staffing of new healthcare jobs with foreigners are slowing development. In the meantime, social investment has led to better living standards, including increased school enrollment, a substantial reduction in infant and child mortality, and greater access to potable water and sanitation.

Since CHAVEZ came to power in 1999, more than a million predominantly middle- and upper-class Venezuelans are estimated to have emigrated. The brain drain is attributed to a repressive political system, lack of economic opportunities, steep inflation, a high crime rate, and corruption. Thousands of oil engineers emigrated to Canada, Colombia, and the United States following CHAVEZ's firing of over 20,000 employees of the state-owned petroleum company during a 2002-2003 oil strike. Additionally, thousands of Venezuelans of European descent have taken up residence in their ancestral homelands. Nevertheless, Venezuela continues to attract immigrants from South America and southern Europe because of its lenient migration policy and the availability of education and healthcare. Venezuela also has been a fairly accommodating host to more than 200,000 Colombian refugees.

**Population:**
28,459,085 (July 2013 est.)

country comparison to the world: 45

**Age structure:**
0-14 years: 28.6% (male 4,144,958/female 3,989,521)

15-24 years: 18.8% (male 2,686,366/female 2,664,062)

25-54 years: 39.5% (male 5,520,689/female 5,727,432)

55-64 years: 7.3% (male 993,176/female 1,094,586)

65 years and over: 5.8% (male 722,234/female 916,061) (2013 est.)

**Median age:**
total: 26.6 years

male: 25.9 years

female: 27.3 years (2013 est.)

**Population growth rate:**
1.44% (2013 est.)

country comparison to the world: 83

**Birth rate:**
19.66 births/1,000 population (2013 est.)

country comparison to the world: 88

**Death rate:**
> 5.23 deaths/1,000 population (2013 est.)
> country comparison to the world: 180

**Net migration rate:**
> 0 migrant(s)/1,000 population (2013 est.)
> country comparison to the world: 78

**Urbanization:**
> urban population: 93% of total population (2010)
> rate of urbanization: 1.7% annual rate of change (2010-15 est.)

**Major urban areas - population:**
> CARACAS (capital) 3.051 million; Maracaibo 2.153 million; Valencia 1.738 million; Barquisimeto 1.159 million; Maracay 1.04 million (2009)

**Sex ratio:**
> at birth: 1.05 male(s)/female
> 0-14 years: 1.04 male(s)/female
> 15-24 years: 1.01 male(s)/female
> 25-54 years: 0.96 male(s)/female
> 55-64 years: 0.91 male(s)/female
> 65 years and over: 0.79 male(s)/female
> total population: 0.98 male(s)/female (2013 est.)

**Maternal mortality rate:**
> 92 deaths/100,000 live births (2010)

country comparison to the world: 78

**Infant mortality rate:**
total: 19.75 deaths/1,000 live births
country comparison to the world: 94
male: 23.18 deaths/1,000 live births
female: 16.14 deaths/1,000 live births (2013 est.)

**Life expectancy at birth:**
total population: 74.23 years
country comparison to the world: 113
male: 71.12 years
female: 77.5 years (2013 est.)

**Total fertility rate:**
2.37 children born/woman (2013 est.)
country comparison to the world: 92

**Contraceptive prevalence rate:**
70.3% (1998)

**Health expenditures:**
4.9% of GDP (2010)
country comparison to the world: 144

**Physicians density:**
1.94 physicians/1,000 population (2001)

**Hospital bed density:**
1.1 beds/1,000 population (2009)

**Drinking water source:**

  improved:
    *urban*: 94% of population
    *rural*: 74% of population
    *total*: 92% of population
  unimproved:
    *urban*: 6% of population
    *rural*: 26% of population
    *total*: 8% of population (2000 est.)

**Sanitation facility access:**
  improved:
    *urban*: 93% of population
    *rural*: 54% of population
    *total*: 89% of population
  unimproved:
    *urban*: 7% of population
    *rural*: 46% of population
    *total*: 11% of population (2000 est.)

**HIV/AIDS - adult prevalence rate:**
  NA; note - no country specific models provided

**HIV/AIDS - people living with HIV/AIDS:**
  NA

**HIV/AIDS - deaths:**
  NA

**Major infectious diseases:**

degree of risk: high

food or waterborne diseases: bacterial diarrhea and hepatitis A

vectorborne diseases: dengue fever and malaria (2013)

**Obesity - adult prevalence rate:**

30.3% (2008)

country comparison to the world: 26

**Children under the age of 5 years underweight:**

3.7% (2007)

country comparison to the world: 98

**Education expenditures:**

3.6% of GDP (2007)

country comparison to the world: 124

**Literacy:**

definition: age 15 and over can read and write

total population: 93%

male: 93.3%

female: 92.7% (2001 census)

**School life expectancy (primary to tertiary education):**

total: 14.3 years (2009)

**Child labor - children ages 5-14:**

total number: 404,092

percentage: 8 % (2000 est.)

**Unemployment, youth ages 15-24:**
    total: 17.5%
    country comparison to the world: 72
    male: 15.1%
    female: 22% (2011)

## Chapter 4: Government and Key Leaders

**Country name:**
> conventional long form: Bolivarian Republic of Venezuela
> conventional short form: Venezuela
> local long form: Republica Bolivariana de Venezuela
> local short form: Venezuela

**Government type:**
> federal republic

**Capital:**
> name: Caracas
> geographic coordinates: 10 29 N, 66 52 W
> time difference: UTC-4.5 (half an hour ahead of Washington, DC during Standard Time)

**Administrative divisions:**
> 23 states (estados, singular - estado), 1 capital district* (distrito capital), and 1 federal dependency** (dependencia federal); Amazonas, Anzoategui, Apure, Aragua, Barinas, Bolivar, Carabobo, Cojedes, Delta Amacuro, Dependencias Federales (Federal Dependencies)**, Distrito Capital (Capital District)*, Falcon, Guarico, Lara, Merida, Miranda, Monagas,

Nueva Esparta, Portuguesa, Sucre, Tachira, Trujillo, Vargas, Yaracuy, Zulia

<u>note</u>: the federal dependency consists of 11 federally controlled island groups with a total of 72 individual islands

**Independence:**

5 July 1811 (from Spain)

**National holiday:**

Independence Day, 5 July (1811)

**Constitution:**

30 December 1999; amended 15 February 2009

**Legal system:**

civil law system based on the Spanish civil code

**International law organization participation:**

has not submitted an ICJ jurisdiction declaration; state party to the ICCT

**Suffrage:**

18 years of age; universal

**Executive branch:**

<u>chief of state</u>: President Nicolas MADURO Moros (since 8 March 2013); Executive Vice President Jorge Alberto ARREAZA Montserrat (since 8 March 2013); note - the president is both chief of state and head of government; former Executive Vice President

Nicolas MADURO Moros assumed presidential responsibilites after the death of President Hugo CHAVEZ Frias on 5 March 2013, and was officially sworn in on 8 March 2013

head of government: President Nicolas MADURO Moros (since 8 March 2013); Executive Vice President Jorge Alberto ARREAZA Montserrat (since 8 March 2013)

cabinet: Council of Ministers appointed by the president

elections: president elected by popular vote for a six-year term (eligible for unlimited reelection); election last held on 14 April 2013; note - this was a special election held following the death of President Hugo CHAVEZ Frias on 5 March 2013; the next scheduled election after this is expected to be held in October 2018 pending official convocation by the country's electoral body)

note: in 1999, a National Constituent Assembly drafted a new constitution that increased the presidential term to six years; an election was subsequently held on 30 July 2000 under the terms of this constitution; in 2009, a national referendum approved the elimination of term limits on all elected officials, including the presidency

election results: Nicolas MADURO Moros elected president; percent of vote - Nicolas MADURO Moros 50.08%, Henrique CAPRILES Radonski 49%, other 0.92%; note - official results pending

**Legislative branch:**

unicameral National Assembly or Asamblea Nacional (165 seats; members elected by popular vote on a proportional basis to serve five-year terms; three seats reserved for the indigenous peoples of Venezuela)

elections: last held on 26 September 2010 (next to be held in 2015)

election results: percent of vote by party - pro-government 48.9%, opposition coalition 47.9%, other 3.2%; seats by party - pro-government 98, opposition 65, other 2

**Judicial branch:**

highest court(s): Supreme Tribunal of Justice (consists of 32 judges organized into six divisions - constitutional, political administrative, electoral, civil appeals, criminal appeals, and social (mainly agrarian and labor issues) judge selection and term of office: judges proposed by the Committee of Judicial Postulation (an independent body of organizations dealing with legal issues and of the organs of citizen power) and appointed by the National Assembly; judges serve non-renewable 12-year terms

<u>subordinate courts</u>: Superior or Appeals Courts (Tribunales Superiores); District Tribunals (Tribunales de Distrito); Courts of First Instance (Tribunales de Primera Instancia); Parish Courts (Tribunales de Parroquia); Justices of the Peace (Justicia de Paz) Network

**Political parties and leaders:**

A New Time or UNT [Omar BARBOZA]

Brave People's Alliance or ABP [Antonio LEDEZMA]

Christian Democrats or COPEI [Roberto ENRIQUEZ]

Communist Party of Venezuela or PCV [Oscar FIGUERA]

Democratic Action or AD [Henry RAMOS ALLUP]

Fatherland for All or PPT [Rafael UZCATEGUI]

For Social Democracy or PODEMOS [Ismael GARCIA]

Justice First [Julio BORGES]

Movement Toward Socialism or MAS [Nicolas SOSA]

Popular Will or VP [Leopoldo LOPEZ]

Progressive Wave or AP [Henri FALCON]

The Democratic Unity Table or MUD [Ramon Guillermo AVELEDO]

The Radical Cause [Daniel SANTOLO]

United Socialist Party of Venezuela or PSUV [Hugo CHAVEZ]

Venezuelan Progressive Movement or MPV [Simon CALZADILLA]

Venezuela Project or PV [Henrique SALAS ROMER]

**Political pressure groups and leaders:**

Bolivarian and Socialist Workers' Union (a ruling party labor union)

Confederacion Venezolana de Industriales or Coindustria (a conservative business group)

Consejos Comunales (pro-Chavez local cooperatives)

FEDECAMARAS (a conservative business group)

Union of Oil Workers of Venezuela or FUTPV

Venezuelan Confederation of Workers or CTV (opposition-oriented labor organization) various civil society groups and human rights organizations

**International organization participation:**
Caricom (observer), CD, CDB, CELAC, FAO, G-15, G-24, G-77, IADB, IAEA, IBRD, ICAO, ICC (NGOs), ICCt, ICRM, IDA, IFAD, IFC, IFRCS, IHO, ILO, IMF, IMO, IMSO, Interpol, IOC, IOM, IPU, ITSO, ITU, ITUC (NGOs), LAES, LAIA, LAS (observer), Mercosur, MIGA, NAM, OAS, OPANAL, OPCW, OPEC, PCA, Petrocaribe, UN, UNASUR, UNCTAD, UNESCO, UNHCR, UNIDO, Union Latina, UNWTO, UPU, WCO, WFTU (NGOs), WHO, WIPO, WMO, WTO

**Diplomatic representation in the US:**
chief of mission: Ambassador (vacant); Charge d'Affaires Calixto Antonio ORTEGA Rios
chancery: 1099 30th Street NW, Washington, DC 20007
telephone: [1] (202) 342-2214
FAX: [1] (202) 342-6820
consulate(s) general: Boston, Chicago, Houston, Miami, New Orleans, New York, San Francisco, San Juan (Puerto Rico)

**Diplomatic representation from the US:**

chief of mission: Ambassador (vacant); Charge d'Affaires James M. DERHAM

embassy: Calle F con Calle Suapure, Urbanizacion Colinas de Valle Arriba, Caracas 1080

mailing address: P. O. Box 62291, Caracas 1060-A; APO AA 34037

telephone: [58] (212) 975-6411, 907-8400 (after hours)

FAX: [58] (212) 907-8199

**Key Leaders:**

| | |
|---|---|
| Pres. | **Nicolas MADURO Moros** |
| Executive Vice Pres. | **Jorge Alberto ARREAZA Montserrat** |
| Min. of Agriculture & Lands | **Yvan GIL** |
| Min. of Air & Water Transportation | **Herbert GARCIA Plaza** |
| Min. of Commerce | **Alejandro FLEMING** |
| Min. of Communal Affairs | **Reinaldo ITURRIZA** |
| Min. of Communications & Information | **Ernesto VILLEGAS** |
| Min. of Culture | **Fidel BARBARITO** |
| Min. of Defense | **Diego MOLERO Bellavia** |
| Min. of Education | **Maryann del Carmen** |

| | |
|---|---|
| | HANSON Flores |
| Min. of Electricity | Jesse CHACON |
| Min. of Environment & Natural Resources | Dante RIVAS |
| Min. of Finance | Nelson Jose MERENTES Diaz |
| Min. of Foreign Affairs | Elias Jose JAUA Milano |
| Min. of Ground Transportation | Haiman EL TROUDI |
| Min. of Higher Education | Pedro CALZADILLA |
| Min. of Housing & Habitats | Ricardo Antonio MOLINA Penaloza |
| Min. of Indigenous Peoples | Aloha NUNEZ |
| Min. of Industry | Ricardo MENENDEZ |
| Min. of Interior, Justice, & Peace | Miguel RODRIGUEZ Torres |
| Min. of Labor & Social Security | Maria Cristina IGLESIAS |
| Min. of Nutrition | Felix OSORIO |
| Min. of the Office of the Presidency & Govt. Performance Monitoring | Carmen MELENDEZ |

| | |
|---|---|
| Min. of Penitentiary Services | Maria Iris VARELA Rangel |
| Min. of Petroleum & Mining | Rafael Dario RAMIREZ Carreno |
| Min. of Planning | Jorge Antonio GIORDANI Cordero |
| Min. of Public Health & Social Development | Isabel ITURRIA |
| Min. of Science & Technology | Manuel FERNANDEZ |
| Min. of Sports | Alejandra BENITEZ |
| Min. of Tourism | Andres IZARRA |
| Min. of Women's Affairs | Andreina TARAZON |
| Min. of Youth | Hector RODRIGUEZ |
| Prosecutor Gen. | Luisa ORTEGA Diaz |
| Pres., Central Bank | Edmee BETANCOURT |
| Charge d'Affaires, Embassy, Washington | Calixto Antonio ORTEGA Rios |
| Permanent Representative to the UN, New York | Jorge Hidalgo VALERO Briceno |

**Flag description:**

three equal horizontal bands of yellow (top), blue, and red with the coat of arms on the hoist side of the yellow band and an arc of eight white five-pointed stars centered in the blue band; the flag retains the three equal horizontal bands and three main colors of the banner of Gran Colombia, the South American republic that broke up in 1830; yellow is interpreted as standing for the riches of the land, blue for the courage of its people, and red for the blood shed in attaining independence; the seven stars on the original flag represented the seven provinces in Venezuela that united in the war of independence; in 2006, President Hugo CHAVEZ ordered an eighth star added to the star arc - a decision that sparked much controversy - to conform with the flag proclaimed by Simon Bolivar in 1827 and to represent the province of Guayana

**National symbol(s):**
troupial (bird)

**National anthem:**
name: "Gloria al bravo pueblo" (Glory to the Brave People)
lyrics/music: Vicente SALIAS/Juan Jose LANDAETA
note: adopted 1881; the lyrics were written in 1810, the music some years later; both SALIAS and

LANDAETA were executed in 1814 during Venezuela's struggle for independence

# Chapter 5: Economy

**Economy - overview:**

Venezuela remains highly dependent on oil revenues, which account for roughly 95% of export earnings, about 45% of federal budget revenues, and around 12% of GDP. Fueled by high oil prices, record government spending helped to boost GDP growth by 4.2% in 2011, after a sharp drop in oil prices caused an economic contraction in 2009-10. Government spending, minimum wage hikes, and improved access to domestic credit created an increase in consumption which combined with supply problems to cause higher inflation - roughly 26% in 2011 and 21% in 2012. President Hugo CHAVEZ's efforts to increase the government's control of the economy by nationalizing firms in the agribusiness, financial, construction, oil, and steel sectors have hurt the private investment environment, reduced productive capacity, and slowed non-petroleum exports. In the first half of 2010 Venezuela faced the prospect of lengthy nationwide blackouts when its main hydroelectric power plant - which provides more than 35% of the country's electricity - nearly shut down. In

May 2010, CHAVEZ closed the unofficial foreign exchange market - the "parallel market" - in an effort to stem inflation and slow the currency's depreciation. In June 2010, the government created the "Transaction System for Foreign Currency Denominated Securities" to replace the "parallel" market. In December 2010, CHAVEZ eliminated the dual exchange rate system and unified the exchange rate at 4.3 bolivars per dollar. In January 2011, CHAVEZ announced the second devaluation of the bolivar within twelve months. In December 2010, the National Assembly passed a package of five organic laws designed to complete the transformation of the Venezuelan economy in line with CHAVEZ's vision of 21st century socialism. In 2012, Venezuela continued to wrestle with a housing crisis, high inflation, an electricity crisis, and rolling food and goods shortages - all of which were fallout from the government's unorthodox economic policies. The budget deficit for the entire government reached 17% of GDP in 2012, and public debt as a percent of GDP climbed steeply to 49%, despite record oil prices.

**GDP (purchasing power parity):**
$408.5 billion (2012 est.)

country comparison to the world: 34
$387.1 billion (2011 est.)
$371.5 billion (2010 est.)
note: data are in 2012 US dollars

**GDP (official exchange rate):**
$382.4 billion (2012 est.)

**GDP - real growth rate:**
5.5% (2012 est.)
country comparison to the world: 52
4.2% (2011 est.)
-1.5% (2010 est.)

**GDP - per capita (PPP):**
$13,800 (2012 est.)
country comparison to the world: 97
$13,300 (2011 est.)
$13,000 (2010 est.)
note: data are in 2012 US dollars

**GDP - composition by sector:**
agriculture: 3.7%
industry: 35.5%
services: 60.8% (2012 est.)

**Labor force:**
13.49 million (2012 est.)
country comparison to the world: 41

**Labor force - by occupation:**

agriculture: 7.3%

industry: 21.8%

services: 70.9% (4th quarter, 2011 est.)

**Unemployment rate:**

7.8% (2012 est.)

country comparison to the world: 88

8.2% (2011 est.)

**Population below poverty line:**

31.6% (2011 est.)

**Household income or consumption by percentage share:**

lowest 10%: 1.7%

highest 10%: 32.7% (2006)

**Distribution of family income - Gini index:**

39 (2011)

country comparison to the world: 69

49.5 (1998)

**Investment (gross fixed):**

19.9% of GDP (2012 est.)

country comparison to the world: 95

**Budget:**

revenues: $109.8 billion

expenditures: $165.3 billion (2012 est.)

**Taxes and other revenues:**

28.7% of GDP (2012 est.)

country comparison to the world: 102

**Budget surplus (+) or deficit (-):**

-14.5% of GDP (2012 est.)

country comparison to the world: 214

**Public debt:**

26.8% of GDP (2012 est.)

country comparison to the world: 121

25.1% of GDP (2011 est.)

note: data cover central government debt, as well as the debt of state-owned oil company PDVSA; the data include treasury debt held by foreign entities; the data include some debt issued by subnational entities, as well as intra-governmental debt; intra-governmental debt consists of treasury borrowings from surpluses in the social funds, such as for retirement, medical care, and unemployment; some debt instruments for the social funds are sold at public auctions

**Inflation rate (consumer prices):**

21.1% (2012 est.)

country comparison to the world: 216

26.1% (2011 est.)

**Central bank discount rate:**

29.5% (31 December 2010)

country comparison to the world: 3

29.5% (31 December 2009)

**Commercial bank prime lending rate:**

16.38% (31 December 2012 est.)

country comparison to the world: 28

17.15% (31 December 2011 est.)

**Stock of narrow money:**

$163 billion (31 December 2012 est.)

country comparison to the world: 23

$110.8 billion (31 December 2011 est.)

**Stock of broad money:**

$188.2 billion (31 December 2012 est.)

country comparison to the world: 43

$115.9 billion (31 December 2011 est.)

**Stock of domestic credit:**

$147.1 billion (31 December 2012 est.)

country comparison to the world: 45

$92.82 billion (31 December 2011 est.)

**Market value of publicly traded shares:**

$5.143 billion (31 December 2011)

country comparison to the world: 89

$3.991 billion (31 December 2010)

$8.86 billion (31 December 2010)

**Agriculture - products:**
    corn, sorghum, sugarcane, rice, bananas, vegetables, coffee; beef, pork, milk, eggs; fish

**Industries:**
    petroleum, construction materials, food processing, textiles; iron ore mining, steel, aluminum; motor vehicle assembly, chemical products, paper products

**Industrial production growth rate:**
    4.7% (2012 est.)
    country comparison to the world: 58

**Current account balance:**
    $20.6 billion (2012 est.)
    country comparison to the world: 18
    $27.21 billion (2011 est.)

**Exports:**
    $97.34 billion (2012 est.)
    country comparison to the world: 40
    $92.81 billion (2011 est.)

**Exports - commodities:**
    petroleum, bauxite and aluminum, minerals, chemicals, agricultural products, basic manufactures

**Exports - partners:**
    US 39.3%, China 14.4%, India 12%, Netherlands Antilles 7.6%, Cuba 4.5% (2012)

**Imports:**
$59.31 billion (2012 est.)
country comparison to the world: 50
$46.78 billion (2011 est.)

**Imports - commodities:**
agricultural products, livestock, raw materials, machinery and equipment, transport equipment, construction materials, medical equipment, pharmaceuticals, chemicals, iron and steel products

**Imports - partners:**
US 31.2%, China 16.5%, Brazil 8.9% (2012)

**Reserves of foreign exchange and gold:**
$29.89 billion (31 December 2012 est.)
country comparison to the world: 51
$29.89 billion (31 December 2011 est.)

**Debt - external:**
$75.75 billion (31 December 2012 est.)
country comparison to the world: 53
$67.91 billion (31 December 2011 est.)

**Stock of direct foreign investment - at home:**
$47.4 billion (31 December 2012 est.)
country comparison to the world: 55
$45.2 billion (31 December 2011 est.)

**Stock of direct foreign investment - abroad:**

$21.25 billion (31 December 2012 est.)

country comparison to the world: 45

$19.81 billion (31 December 2011 est.)

**Exchange rates:**

bolivars (VEB) per US dollar

4.289 (2012 est.)

4.289 (2011 est.)

2.5821 (2010 est.)

2.147 (2009)

2.147 (2008)

**Fiscal year:**

calendar year

# Chapter 6: Energy

**Electricity - production:**
>127.6 billion kWh (2012 est.)
>country comparison to the world: 29

**Electricity - consumption:**
>85.05 billion kWh (2011 est.)
>country comparison to the world: 35

**Electricity - exports:**
>633 million kWh (2009 est.)
>country comparison to the world: 58

**Electricity - imports:**
>260 million kWh (2009 est.)
>country comparison to the world: 85

**Electricity - installed generating capacity:**
>27.5 million kW (2012 est.)
>country comparison to the world: 29

**Electricity - from fossil fuels:**
>35.7% of total installed capacity (2012 est.)
>country comparison to the world: 175

**Electricity - from nuclear fuels:**
>0% of total installed capacity (2012 est.)
>country comparison to the world: 198

**Electricity - from hydroelectric plants:**

64.3% of total installed capacity (2012 est.)

country comparison to the world: 27

**Electricity - from other renewable sources:**

0% of total installed capacity (2012 est.)

country comparison to the world: 200

**Crude oil - production:**

2.47 million bbl/day (2011 est.)

country comparison to the world: 14

**Crude oil - exports:**

1.645 million bbl/day (2010 est.)

country comparison to the world: 10

**Crude oil - imports:**

0 bbl/day (2009 est.)

country comparison to the world: 137

**Crude oil - proved reserves:**

209.4 billion bbl (1 January 2012 est.)

country comparison to the world: 3

**Refined petroleum products - production:**

1.176 million bbl/day (2008 est.)

country comparison to the world: 21

**Refined petroleum products - consumption:**

571,000 bbl/day (2011 est.)

country comparison to the world: 33

**Refined petroleum products - exports:**

638,000 bbl/day (2010 est.)

country comparison to the world: 11

**Refined petroleum products - imports:**

16,660 bbl/day (2011 est.)

country comparison to the world: 112

**Natural gas - production:**

31.2 billion cu m (2011 est.)

country comparison to the world: 28

**Natural gas - consumption:**

33.1 billion cu m (2011 est.)

country comparison to the world: 29

**Natural gas - exports:**

0 cu m (2011 est.)

country comparison to the world: 201

**Natural gas - imports:**

1.446 billion cu m (2011 est.)

country comparison to the world: 53

**Natural gas - proved reserves:**

5.524 trillion cu m (1 January 2012 est.)

country comparison to the world: 9

**Carbon dioxide emissions from consumption of energy:**

158.4 million Mt (2010 est.)

country comparison to the world: 33

# Chapter 7: Communications

**Telephones - main lines in use:**
7.332 million (2011)
country comparison to the world: 24

**Telephones - mobile cellular:**
28.782 million (2011)
country comparison to the world: 35

**Telephone system:**
general assessment: modern and expanding
domestic: domestic satellite system with 3 earth stations; recent substantial improvement in telephone service in rural areas; substantial increase in digitalization of exchanges and trunk lines; installation of a national interurban fiber-optic network capable of digital multimedia services; combined fixed and mobile-cellular telephone subscribership 130 per 100 persons
international: country code - 58; submarine cable systems provide connectivity to the Caribbean, Central and South America, and US; satellite earth stations - 1 Intelsat (Atlantic Ocean) and 1 PanAmSat; participating with Colombia, Ecuador, Peru, and Bolivia in the construction of an

international fiber-optic network; constructing submarine cable to provide connectivity to Cuba with an estimated date of completion in late 2011 (2010)

**Broadcast media:**

government supervises a mixture of state-run and private broadcast media; 1 state-run TV network, 4 privately owned TV networks, a privately owned news channel with limited national coverage, and a government-backed pan-American channel; state-run radio network includes 65 news stations and roughly another 30 stations targeted at specific audiences; state-sponsored community broadcasters include 244 radio stations and 36 TV stations; the number of private broadcast radio stations has been declining, but many still remain in operation (2010)

**Internet country code:**

.ve

**Internet hosts:**

1.016 million (2012)

country comparison to the world: 46

**Internet users:**

8.918 million (2009)

country comparison to the world: 32

# Chapter 8: Transportation

**Airports:**
>492 (2012)
>
>country comparison to the world: 15

**Airports - with paved runways:**
>total: 128
>
>over 3,047 m: 6
>
>2,438 to 3,047 m: 9
>
>1,524 to 2,437 m: 35
>
>914 to 1,523 m: 61
>
>under 914 m: 17 (2012)

**Airports - with unpaved runways:**
>total: 364
>
>2,438 to 3,047 m: 3
>
>1,524 to 2,437 m: 55
>
>914 to 1,523 m: 113
>
>under 914 m: 193 (2012)

**Heliports:**
>3 (2012)

**Pipelines:**
>extra heavy crude 981 km; gas 5,941 km; oil 7,588 km; refined products 1,778 km (2013)

**Railways:**

total: 806 km

country comparison to the world: 98

standard gauge: 806 km 1.435-m gauge (41 km electrified) (2008)

**Roadways:**

total: 96,155 km

country comparison to the world: 44

paved: 32,308 km

unpaved: 63,847 km (2002)

**Waterways:**

7,100 km (the Orinoco River (400 km) and Lake de Maracaibo are navigable by oceangoing vessels) (2011)

country comparison to the world: 21

**Merchant marine:**

total: 53

country comparison to the world: 69

by type: bulk carrier 4, cargo 12, chemical tanker 1, liquefied gas 5, passenger 1, passenger/cargo 14, petroleum tanker 16

foreign-owned: 9 (Denmark 1, Estonia 1, Germany 1, Greece 4, Mexico 1, Spain 1)

registered in other countries: 14 (Panama 13, Saint Vincent and the Grenadines 1) (2010)

**Ports and terminals:**

La Guaira, Maracaibo, Puerto Cabello, Punta Cardon

oil terminals: Jose terminal

**Transportation - note:**

the International Maritime Bureau reports the territorial and offshore waters in the Caribbean Sea as a significant risk for piracy and armed robbery against ships; numerous vessels, including commercial shipping and pleasure craft, have been attacked and hijacked both at anchor and while underway; crews have been robbed and stores or cargoes stolen

# Chapter 9: Military

**Military branches:**
 Bolivarian National Armed Forces (Fuerza Armada Nacional Bolivariana, FANB): Bolivarian Army (Ejercito Bolivariano, EB), Bolivarian Navy (Armada Bolivariana, AB; includes Naval Infantry, Coast Guard, Naval Aviation), Bolivarian Military Aviation (Aviacion Militar Bolivariana, AMB; includes Air National Guard), Bolivarian National Guard (Guardia Nacional Bolivaria, GNB) (2013)

**Military service age and obligation:**
 18-30 years of age for compulsory and voluntary military service; 30-month conscript service obligation; Navy requires 6th-grade education for enlisted personnel; all citizens of military service age (18-60 years old) are obligated to register for military service (2012)

**Manpower available for military service:**
 males age 16-49: 7,013,854
 females age 16-49: 7,165,661 (2010 est.)

**Manpower fit for military service:**
 males age 16-49: 5,614,743
 females age 16-49: 6,074,834 (2010 est.)

**Manpower reaching militarily significant age annually:**
    male: 277,210
    female: 273,353 (2010 est.)

**Military expenditures:**
    0.7% of GDP (2012)
    country comparison to the world: 154

# Chapter 10: Transnational Issues

**Disputes - international:**

claims all of the area west of the Essequibo River in Guyana, preventing any discussion of a maritime boundary; Guyana has expressed its intention to join Barbados in asserting claims before the United Nations Convention on the Law of the Sea that Trinidad and Tobago's maritime boundary with Venezuela extends into their waters; dispute with Colombia over maritime boundary and Venezuelan administered Los Monjes islands near the Gulf of Venezuela; Colombian organized illegal narcotics and paramilitary activities penetrate Venezuela's shared border region; in 2006, an estimated 139,000 Colombians sought protection in 150 communities along the border in Venezuela; US, France, and the Netherlands recognize Venezuela's granting full effect to Aves Island, thereby claiming a Venezuelan Economic Exclusion Zone/continental shelf extending over a large portion of the eastern Caribbean Sea; Dominica, Saint Kitts and Nevis, Saint Lucia, and Saint Vincent and the Grenadines protest Venezuela's full effect claim

**Refugees and internally displaced persons:**
>refugees (country of origin): 201,941 (Colombia) (2011)

**Trafficking in persons:**
>current situation: Venezuela is a source, transit, and destination country for men, women, and children trafficked for the purposes of commercial sexual exploitation and forced labor; Venezuelan women and girls are trafficked within the country for sexual exploitation, lured from the nation's interior to urban and tourist areas; to a lesser extent, Brazilian women and Colombian women are subjected to forced prostitution; some Venezuelan women are transported to Caribbean islands, particularly Aruba, Curacao, and Trinidad & Tobago, where they are subjected to forced prostitution
>
>tier rating: Tier 3 - the government investigated potential cases of suspected human trafficking and arrested at least 12 people for trafficking crimes during the reporting period; however, there was no further publicly available information regarding those cases; Venezuela is not making significant efforts to comply with the minimum standards for the elimination of trafficking (2008)

**Illicit drugs:** small-scale illicit producer of opium and coca for the processing of opiates and coca derivatives; however, large quantities of cocaine, heroin, and marijuana transit the country from Colombia bound for US and Europe; significant narcotics-related money-laundering activity, especially along the border with Colombia and on Margarita Island; active eradication program primarily targeting opium; increasing signs of drug-related activities by Colombian insurgents on border

# Map of Venezuela

# *Other Key Facts™ Titles*

Key Facts on Syria

Key Facts on China

Key Facts on Qatar

Key Facts on India

Key Facts on Germany

Key Facts on Argentina

Key Facts on Russia

Key Facts on North Korea

Key Facts on Brazil

Key Facts on Italy

Key Facts on the United Arab Emirates

Key Facts on the European Union

Key Facts on Pakistan

Key Facts on Saudi Arabia

Key Facts on Cyprus

Key Facts on Iran

Key Facts on Afghanistan

Key Facts on Iraq

Key Facts on Indonesia

Key Facts on South Korea

Key Facts on France

Key Facts on the United Kingdom

Key Facts on Egypt

Key Facts on Israel

Key Facts on Mexico

Key Facts on the United States of America

Key Facts on Turkey

Key Facts on South Africa

Key Facts on Greece

Key Facts on Japan

Key Facts on Malaysia

Key Facts on Vietnam

Key Facts on Hong Kong

Key Facts on Jordan

Key Facts on Australia

All Key Facts™ Titles are Available at www.Amazon.com

THE INTERNATIONALIST®
2013
WWW.INTERNATIONALIST.COM

www.ingramcontent.com/pod-product-compliance
Lightning Source LLC
Chambersburg PA
CBHW071642170526
45166CB00003B/1401